Barefoot Books

WORLD ATLAS

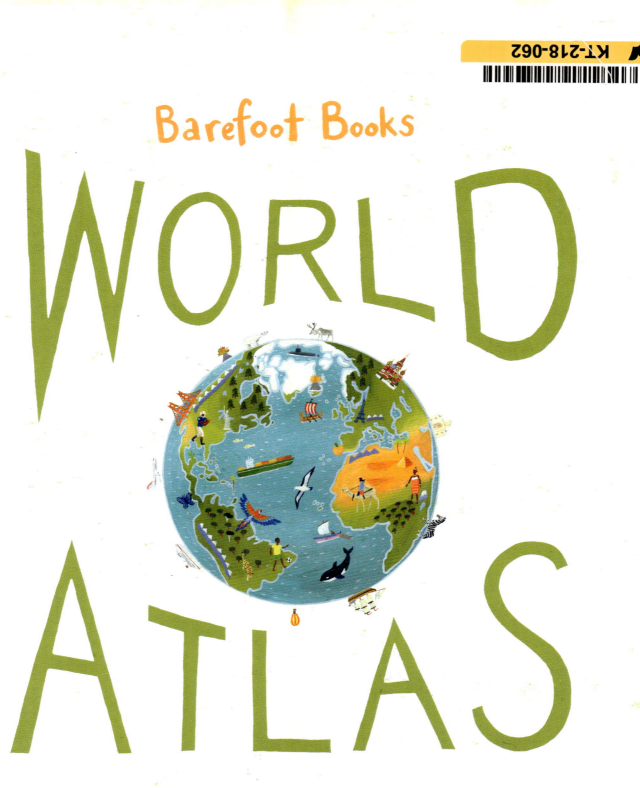

Written by NICK CRANE

Illustrated by DAVID DEAN

Barefoot Books
step inside a story

Contents

The Story of our Planet

The Solar System

An atlas is the most recent chapter of a miracle story. It is a story that began when a small part of the universe collapsed to form a dense core surrounded by a rotating disc of gas and dust particles. Nearly all of the material in the swirling disc ended up being drawn to the core, where it formed a shining sphere, the sun. The scattered grains of remaining material collided with each other and eventually formed the family of planets that we call the solar system, with the sun at its centre.

Pluto

Saturn

Mercury Sun Venus

Neptune

Mars Earth

Jupiter

Uranus

One of these planets, the one third-closest to the sun, was destined to be different. It was so hot that it was molten. When it started to cool, a crust formed on its outside, rather like a cracked shell. Very, very slowly, parts of the crust slid across the surface of the planet. When they collided, their edges sometimes bent and folded into ranges of mountains. Cracks opened up, allowing molten rock to burst upwards as volcanoes of heat and gas, creating new landscapes.

The First Signs of Life

All the while, this ball of spinning rock was being bombarded by meteorites and comets – some of which carried water or ice. Eventually, warm, soupy oceans covered most of the planet's surface, which became wrapped in a thin film of gases – the beginnings of an atmosphere. Nobody knows for sure, but it is likely that the first forms of life, bacteria, developed deep in the planet's scalding interior through a series of chemical reactions. It took ages for the earliest, simplest life forms to migrate from the depths to the bright sunlight of the surface. Bacteria evolved into multicellular organisms, which evolved into plants and worms, fish, amphibians, reptiles, insects, birds and mammals.

The Human Species

When the planet was pulverised by meteorites, or clouded by volcanic eruptions, whole species were wiped out; others adapted. One of these species eventually learnt to run, climb and swim. It also developed a complex mind which was curious about technology, art and music. This species had a sense of what was 'right' and what was 'wrong', spending a lot of time just thinking about things. *Homo sapiens* (a Latin name meaning 'wise human') inherited a planet of incredible diversity. The oceans teemed with fish. The great mountain ranges poured with rivers of crystal water, fed by snowfields and glaciers. Forests reached across entire land masses. When humans learnt to measure time, they discovered that 4,700 million years had passed since their home first started to take shape. We now estimate that our species has been around for only 140,000 years. If you think of the life of the planet as a week, we have been here for less than one minute!

Mapping the World

The Story of Map-Making

The first book of maps to carry the title 'Atlas' was created in the sixteenth century by Gerard Mercator, who was born in Flanders, now Belgium. An atlas is both a precise geometric and an artistic way of representing the different features of the world on paper. The way in which people design atlases is influenced by many factors, including the knowledge they have about the physical features and distances within the different regions; what aspects of life are culturally, economically and politically significant to them; and what geometric techniques they have mastered.

Atlases are a compromise, because it is impossible to flatten the planet, which is a three-dimensional sphere, into two dimensions without distorting the geography. Over the centuries, map-makers, or cartographers, have created new, two-dimensional projections of the earth to try to resolve this problem. Ever since the earliest navigators set sail, we have been making discoveries about our planet and the universe. But no atlas can be accurate for long: the planet is a living, changing place and there is still a lot about it that we do not know.

About this Atlas

The maps in this atlas describe the planet as it is today and illustrate some of the ways in which people in different parts of the world are trying to achieve a better balance between humans and the environment. There is a lot more sea than land on the planet and the sea is far less well known than much of the land.

The first maps in this atlas explore this relatively uncharted territory, from the biggest of the major oceans, the Pacific, to the Southern Ocean. Next, the maps lead you on a journey from east to west, starting in Oceania, where the International Date Line is situated.

Some atlases divide the world by continent. This atlas is divided by region, with an emphasis on the way in which people in different parts of the world have been influenced by the physical characteristics of the land and by the resources around them. Until recently, human beings have lived on the planet in a relatively sustainable way, seldom taking more than can be replaced by natural growth. But in the past century, this balance has changed. Each region has its own story and today some human beings live in a more sustainable way than others, but all of the regions are connected to each other like the pieces of a jigsaw. We are living at the start of a new chapter in the story of our planet and its central theme is the way in which we work together as a global community to protect it.

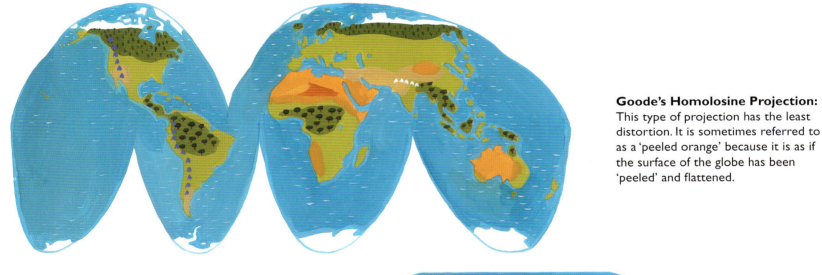

Goode's Homolosine Projection:
This type of projection has the least distortion. It is sometimes referred to as a 'peeled orange' because it is as if the surface of the globe has been 'peeled' and flattened.

Winkel Tripel Projection:
This projection provides a good balance between a globe-like shape and a true representation of the areas of the world. This is the projection used for the world map on the next page.

NORTH
AMERICA

ATLANTIC
OCEAN

PACIFIC
OCEAN

SOUTH
AMERICA

ARCT

CEAN

ASIA

UROPE

AFRICA

INDIAN
OCEAN

OCEANIA

SOUTHERN
OCEAN

ANTARCTICA

The Oceans

Oceans have far more in common with each other than continents, because they are all connected. Currents flow between them, mixing their waters.

You could say that there is just one big ocean. However, people tend to divide them into five: the Pacific, Atlantic, Indian, Arctic and Southern oceans.

The oceans are much more mysterious than land masses. Even today, they are not fully explored. We know that they contain nearly all the water on earth (97%) but we don't know much about life in the oceans. Scientists estimate that they provide a habitat for 80% of life on Earth: perhaps as many as 10 million different species, only 300,000 of them recorded.

Most of the earth's incoming solar radiation is absorbed by the oceans, which store thermal energy extremely effectively. Ocean currents play a major role in distributing heat around the globe, making them key elements in the climate system.

About 73% of the world's fish supply comes from the oceans. Altogether, fish provide some 2.8 billion people with at least a fifth of their protein intake. Since the 1950s, the increasing amounts of fish being caught in our oceans have drastically reduced stocks and threaten to make many species extinct. Today, governments and international organisations are working together to co-ordinate fishing policy and protect fish stocks. However, no single body controls fishing in international waters, so voluntary co-operation between countries and their fishing fleets is essential.

Oceans can be crossed by many different means. Ferdinand Magellan's expedition (1519–22) was the first to sail around the world. His flagship, *Trinidad*, led a fleet of five ships provided by King Charles V. Other pioneering ocean crossings include Charles Lindbergh's solo flight by monoplane in 1927 across the Atlantic Ocean. Amelia Earhart was the first woman to repeat Lindbergh's feat, exactly five years later. In 1981, *Double Eagle V* became the first hot air balloon to cross the Pacific Ocean.

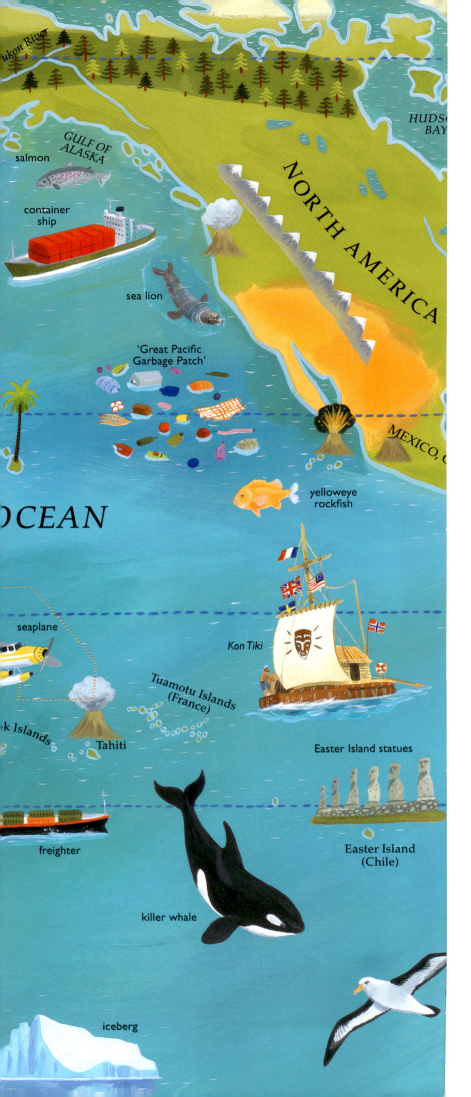

salmon

GULF OF
ALASKA

container
ship

NORTH AMERICA

HUDSON
BAY

sea lion

'Great Pacific
Garbage Patch'

OCEAN

yelloweye
rockfish

MEXICO,

seaplane

Kon Tiki

Tuamotu Islands
(France)

k Islands

Tahiti

Easter Island statues

Easter Island
(Chile)

freighter

killer whale

iceberg

The Pacific Ocean

The largest ocean is the Pacific, which occupies about one-third of the globe. It is greater in extent than the total land area of the world.

Physical Features
The Pacific has over 25,000 islands, which is more than all the other oceans combined, although the islands are mostly tiny. The Asian side of the ocean is broken into huge islands and peninsulas, and into several 'seas': the South China Sea, East China Sea, Yellow Sea, Sea of Japan, Sea of Okhotsk and Bering Sea.

The deepest part of the Pacific is also the lowest point on the planet. Between Japan and New Guinea, where the boundary between two of the earth's crustal plates has created an underwater chasm called the Mariana Trench, the depth is 10,920m. If you dropped Mount Everest into this, it would still be covered by 2,000m of water.

Climate and Weather
Temperatures in the Pacific Ocean range from below 0°C in the polar areas to 30°C at the equator. Periodically, parts of the tropical Pacific warm by a few degrees Celsius, which can have a huge effect on the earth's climate. This phenomenon, called El Niño, can cause extreme weather like floods and droughts in many different parts of the world.

Natural Resources
The Pacific Ocean is home to all kinds of fish, including herring, salmon, sardines, snapper, swordfish and tuna. Many shellfish also live in its waters, as do larger sea creatures such as dolphins, turtles and whales. The ocean has rich reserves of gas and oil, providing energy for Australia, New Zealand, China, Peru and the United States.

Environment
Oil pollution and overfishing threaten many marine species in the Pacific Ocean, particularly whales, turtles, seals, sea otters, sea lions and the strange dugong, or 'sea cow', which eats coastal plants and can live for up to 70 years.

In the north Pacific floats the 'Great Pacific Garbage Patch', which is an enormous area of plastic waste. This kills more than a million seabirds each year and as many marine animals. International efforts are being made to clear it up.

The Atlantic Ocean

The Atlantic Ocean is just over half the size of the Pacific and the second largest of the world's oceans. It reaches from the Arctic Ocean in the north to the Southern Ocean in the south.

Physical Features

Compared to the Pacific, the Atlantic doesn't have many islands, but around its edges there are a number of shallow seas, like the Caribbean, the Gulf of Mexico, the Mediterranean, the Baltic and the Black Sea.

The Atlantic was created when the continents of Africa and North and South America began drifting apart about 130 million years ago. Deep beneath its surface is a mountain range called the Mid-Atlantic Ridge, where molten lava has risen through the rupture in the ocean floor caused by the earth's plates moving apart. Today, the Atlantic Ocean is still growing wider, at a rate of about 2.5cm a year.

Climate and Weather

Sea-surface temperatures in the Atlantic vary. Around the equator, temperatures reach up to 28°C, while in the polar regions they sink to around 7°C. Average temperatures have risen by 0.7°C over the last century.

Ocean currents influence the climate: the Gulf Stream brings warm waters to northwest Europe, while cold currents create dense fog off the coasts of eastern Canada and northwest Africa.

Natural Resources

The Atlantic is the world's richest source of fish. Common species are cod, haddock, hake, herring and mackerel. The rocks below the ocean bed are rich in oil and gas, and sand and gravel banks provide raw materials for the building industry.

Environment

To the west and east of the Atlantic are the two continents — North America and Europe — which have emitted well over half of the world's greenhouse gases. The major greenhouse gases generated by human activity are carbon dioxide and methane. Growth in atmospheric carbon concentration (over 25% since the mid 1800s) is mainly due to our use of fossil fuels.

The oceans play a vital role in absorbing carbon dioxide and maintaining the planet's 'carbon balance'. Half of the carbon dioxide generated by human beings since 1800 has been absorbed by the sea. However, so much carbon dioxide is being absorbed by the oceans that it is increasing the acidity of the water and destroying many forms of marine life.

Did You Know?

Marine Life

There are nearly 6 million Atlantic puffins in the North Atlantic. Atlantic puffins can fly and swim, sometimes diving over 60m underwater to catch the small fish they eat. Although penguins are also birds, they cannot fly. Millions of Magellanic penguins live along the coasts of Argentina and Chile, but they are still classified as a threatened species due to the oil spills that kill thousands each year off the coast of Argentina.

Transport

Transatlantic exploration has brought European and African culture to the Americas. Over 1,000 years ago, Icelander Leif Ericson was the first European to discover North America's coastline. In 1952, Ann Davison became the first woman to sail across the Atlantic single-handed in her 7-metre boat, *Felicity Ann*. Hundreds of commercial flights cross the Atlantic every day, and the ocean continues to be a major route for sea freight.

ARCTIC OCEAN

Arctic Circle

HUDSON
BAY

Viking ship

NORTH SEA

BALTIC
SEA

EUROPE

NORTH AMERICA

puffin

Titanic

haddock

BLACK SEA

MEDITERRANEAN SEA

Tropic of Cancer

Mississippi River

GULF OF
MEXICO

Felicity Ann

Mid-Atlantic Ridge

school of
common
dolphins

NORTH
AFRICA

Nile River

Niger River

CARIBBEAN SEA

ATLANTIC
OCEAN

fishing
boat

Equator

Amazon River

Paraná River

São Francisco River

Equator

Congo River

SOUTHERN
AFRICA

Mid-Atlantic Ridge

SOUTH
AMERICA

passenger
aeroplane

black-browed
albatross

Zambezi River

container ship

Tropic of Capricorn

SOUTHERN OCEAN

blue whale

bottlenose
dolphin

Magellanic
penguin

arctic tern

Antarctic Circle

cruise liner

The Indian Ocean

The Indian Ocean is just under half the size of the Pacific and is enclosed on three sides by the continents of Africa, Asia and Australia.

Physical Features

The Indian Ocean is split into three basins by an underwater mountain range which is known as an oceanic ridge. The ridge was formed millions of years ago by the meeting of three of the earth's crustal plates. At 7,260m deep, the Java Trench is the deepest point of this ocean. Madagascar, which lies to the east of the coast of Africa, is the fourth-largest island in the world.

Did You Know?

Climate and Weather

Much of the Indian Ocean lies in the tropics, so it is the warmest of the oceans. Its tropical climate has a strong effect on the surrounding continents. During the seasonal monsoons, moist air collects over the ocean and falls as torrential rain in countries like Pakistan, India and Bangladesh. Northeast India is the rainiest place on Earth, while high temperatures have turned the Red Sea into one of the saltiest seas in the world.

Natural Resources

Around 40% of the world's offshore oil production is based in the Indian Ocean. As a consequence, marine life in the Arabian Sea, the Persian Gulf and the Red Sea is being affected by pollution from the oil wells.

The Indian Ocean region has the largest number of active fishermen in the world. There is a wide range of marine life for fishermen to catch, including tuna, sardines and shrimp. Attracted by the wealth from oil and fishing, piracy has increased on the Indian Ocean, although governments from around the globe are working together to make the ocean safer for merchants.

Environment

The warming of the oceans through climate change will have a particularly high impact in the Indian Ocean. As the temperature of the oceans rises, their volume increases too, causing sea levels to rise. This means that the many people who live on the low-lying shores of the Indian Ocean may have to move inland.

Marine Life

The warm water of the Indian Ocean is less suitable for marine life than that of the cooler oceans, because there are fewer nutrients for the microscopic plants known as phytoplankton, which are the beginning of the marine food chain. Many whale sharks live in the warm waters of the Indian Ocean, though they migrate all over the world. These sharks feed primarily on plankton. They are the largest fish in the sea, sometimes over 12m long, the size of an average bus.

Whale sharks are a threatened species, as is the dugong, a large mammal that may have inspired the earliest mermaid tales. Dugongs look similar to manatees and are an easy target for coastal hunters who seek their meat and oil. Other species in danger of extinction are seals, turtles and whales.

Transport

For thousands of years, the Indian Ocean has been a water highway between Africa and Asia. The traditional trading vessel in the western part of the ocean was the Arabian dhow, a slender wooden craft with a triangular, lateen sail. By contrast, today's merchant ships, which carry containers, are powered by fossil fuels rather than relying on wind and current. A huge increase in worldwide trade has meant increases in carbon emissions from shipping. In 2005, twice as much food was traded around the world as in 1990.

The Arctic Ocean

The Arctic is by far the smallest and shallowest of the world's oceans; it is 18 times smaller than the Pacific with an average depth of 1,050m. It is almost completely surrounded by north America, Europe and north Asia.

Physical Features

The centre of the Arctic Ocean is occupied by a layer of ice about 3m thick. The Arctic is not as cold as Antarctica, because the seawater beneath the Arctic ice is warmer than the land beneath the Antarctic ice. The Arctic Ocean is connected to the Pacific by the 53km-wide Bering Strait, and to the Atlantic by the much broader Greenland Sea.

The northernmost point on Earth, the North Pole, is about 700km from the coast of northern Greenland. Most of this ice is continuously in motion, breaking into different pieces and drifting around. In 1937, the Soviet Union launched the first temporary drift ice station, 'North Pole-1,' which allowed them to explore the Arctic without needing to leave the base. The drift stations research ice, oceanology, marine biology, meteorology and more.

Climate and Weather

The Arctic Ocean is a region of dark, cold winters and short, cool summers: in summer, temperatures rise to 0°C and in winter they fall to -40°C. At the North Pole, the sun is permanently below the horizon during the winter months and permanently above it during the summer months.

Natural Resources

Oil and gas companies are considering tapping into the rich resources of the Arctic seabed, where there may be as much as 13% of the world's undiscovered oil and 30% of its undiscovered gas. Sand and gravel aggregates, as well as fish, can all be found in abundance in the Arctic Ocean.

Environment

Of all the oceans, the Arctic is most affected by climate change. In recent decades, some parts of the Arctic Ocean have warmed by more than 3°C. Almost half the ice has disappeared since satellite observations began in 1979, and scientists warn that by 2040, the entire ocean may be free of ice in summer. The disappearance of the Arctic ice will affect the ocean's fragile ecosystem and will also accelerate global warming because open water absorbs heat from the sun, whereas ice reflects it back. So, taking action to reduce climate change is vital to the survival of the many species that live in and around the Arctic.

Did You Know?

Wildlife

Many creatures have adapted to the Arctic climate. Polar bears have large, furry feet to help distribute their weight on thin ice, while their white fur has hollow hairs, which trap air and help insulate them from the cold. A less familiar Arctic mammal is the narwhal, also known as the 'unicorn whale' due to its six-foot-long tusk.

Snowy owls live on the Arctic tundra but are unlike other owls as they hunt during the day instead of at night. In the winter, snowy owls are completely white, but their plumage changes to brown in the summer, acting as camouflage. Other animals inhabiting the Arctic include snow geese, tundra swans, peregrine falcons, grizzly bears, musk oxen, grey wolves and arctic foxes.

Transport

The Northwest Passage is a route through the Arctic which links the Atlantic and the Pacific. After several unsuccessful attempts in the nineteenth century, the Passage was finally navigated in 1906 by the explorer Roald Amundsen in a 47-ton fishing boat, the *Gjøa*. He and his crew spent three successive winters trapped in pack ice.

PACIFIC OCEAN

killer whale

GULF OF ALASKA

BERING SEA

SEA OF OKHOTSK

NORTH ASIA

peregrine falcon

Yukon River

Yup'ik mask

BERING STRAIT

snowy owl

harp seal

Nenets people

CHUKCHI SEA

Trans-Alaskan pipeline

NORTH AMERICA

kenzie River

BEAUFORT SEA

Summer Ice

EAST SIBERIAN SEA

River

submarine

tundra swan

polar bear

ARCTIC OCEAN

Summer Ice

LAPTEV SEA

reindeer

Gjøa

Arctic drift station

musk ox

Wally Herbert

icebreaker

Severnaya Zemlya (Russia)

Yenisey River

snow goose

North Pole

Fram

walrus

KARA SEA

Novaya Zemlya (Russia)

arctic fox

Baffin Island (Canada)

BAFFIN BAY

Summer Ice

BARENTS SEA

Svalbard (Norway)

grey wolf

GREENLAND

narwhal

Inuit girl

GREENLAND SEA

Winter Ice

ter Ice

Arctic Circle

Nuuk

Uummannaq

beluga whale

Winter Ice

NORWEGIAN SEA

ATLANTIC OCEAN

ICELAND

EUROPE

The world's second-smallest continent is almost twice the size of the United States, but it has the population of a village.

Physical Features

Antarctica is a land of ice. In places, the ice is nearly 5,000m thick, and in total it accounts for about 90% of the world's fresh water. Less than 1% of Antarctica is free of ice. Buried beneath the ice are entire mountain ranges. Antarctica is the highest continent on Earth, which is one of the reasons that it is so cold and windy. The Southern Ocean was formed when Antarctica and South America moved apart about 30 million years ago.

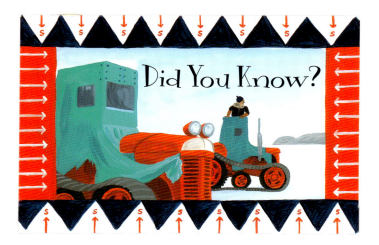

Did You Know?

Climate and Weather

The annual mean temperature on the Antarctic Plateau is around -56°C, which makes it the coldest place in the world. It is also the windiest, with wind speeds on the coast reaching 320kph during gales. Rising sea temperatures have caused the peninsula to become 3°C warmer over the last 50 years. Antarctica is also the world's driest continent: there are places where rain has not fallen for 2 million years.

Natural Resources

Antarctica has reserves of coal, gas and iron ore. Mining is prohibited under the Antarctic Treaty of 1959. Some of its waters are fished for krill, finfish and crab, but quotas are carefully controlled.

Environment

Nobody owns Antarctica. Under the terms of the Antarctic Treaty, the entire continent is a peaceful, non-militarised land open to scientific research and controlled tourism. As one of the world's most important natural laboratories, it is vital to understanding the planet's ocean and climate systems. It is the only continent that has never been permanently settled by human beings, but up to 5,000 scientists occupy a scattering of research stations, mostly on the coast. The most isolated of these stations is the Vostok Station, founded in 1957. It sits on top of a large subglacial lake, which is under 4,000 metres of ice.

By drilling 4km into the Antarctic ice, scientists have been able to obtain a record of the earth's climate going back 800,000 years. These records show that the level of carbon dioxide released into the earth's atmosphere has soared dramatically since the Industrial Revolution. Greenhouse gases (such as carbon dioxide) trap heat in the atmosphere, causing a rise in the earth's temperature. This is known as global warming or the greenhouse effect.

Wildlife

The creature most often associated with Antarctica is the penguin. Of the 17 species of penguin in the world, 4 breed in Antarctica: the Adélie, emperor, chinstrap and gentoo penguins. Penguins cannot fly but they are superb swimmers. They spend about 75% of their time in the water but they breed on land or on sea ice in huge colonies known as 'rookeries'.

The other notable bird of this region is the albatross. These large sea birds are able to cover huge distances without resting. The great albatross has the widest wingspan of any extant bird. Albatrosses are under threat due to overfishing, pollution and also longline fishing.

Transport

The extremely low temperatures and continuous winds make travelling in Antarctica especially difficult. Transport is further limited by environmental concerns: it is important to avoid disrupting the ecosystem or polluting the region. Today, most transport is conducted via water or air, though skis, snowshoes and snowmobiles are also used for overland travel.

Patagonian toothfish

SCOTIA SEA

Antarctic petrel

SOUTHERN OCEAN

emperor penguin

lantern fish

South Shetland Islands (UK)

Antarctic Circle

WEDDELL SEA

leopard seals

dog-sled team

Summer Ice

FILCHNER
ICE SHELF

ANTARCTICA

Antarctic Peninsula

RONNE
ICE SHELF

Roald
Amundsen

converted tractors

crab

South Pole

Antarctic Plateau

Vostok Station

Adélie penguins

AMUNDSEN SEA

ROSS
ICE SHELF

Transantarctic Mountains

krill

Mt. Erebus

ROSS SEA

polar transport
vehicle

Winter Ice

SOUTHERN

southern right
whale

albatross

OCEAN

cruise ship

mackerel icefish

Oceania

If you spin a globe until it looks as if it's mostly covered by sea, you'll be looking at Oceania. Only 33 million people live here — 20 million of them in Australia, 3.7 million in New Zealand and 9.3 million in the islands of the South Pacific.

Pacific Islands

Physical Features

There are between 20,000 and 30,000 islands in the Pacific. New Guinea is the largest landmass in the area, covering 786,000km^2, though half of it extends into southeast Asia. At the other end of the scale, there are numerous uninhabited coral atolls and mountainous islands covered in lush, tropical rainforest.

People and Places

The small islands of Oceania are incredibly varied. The tribal groups of Papua New Guinea speak 820 different languages, while the Federated States of Micronesia occupy 607 islands. Suva is the capital and largest city of Fiji.

Climate and Weather

The weather in this region is tropical all year round, with a hotter and more humid period between November and April, which is also hurricane season.

Natural Resources and Marine Life

For the islanders of Oceania, the sea life of the Pacific Ocean is a major source of food and trade. Many people continue to fish and farm in a traditional way, but modern fishing methods have significantly reduced fish stocks, especially tuna.

The seas of Oceania are host to numerous species of fish and to many types of whale, shark and other sea creatures. This is also a region of spectacular coral reefs.

Environment

The Pacific Ocean is currently shrinking because of the movement of the earth's plates. Many of the islands in this region are low-lying, making them particularly vulnerable to rising sea levels. The increasing temperatures across the southern hemisphere mean that many of the smaller islands in Oceania may disappear within the next few decades.

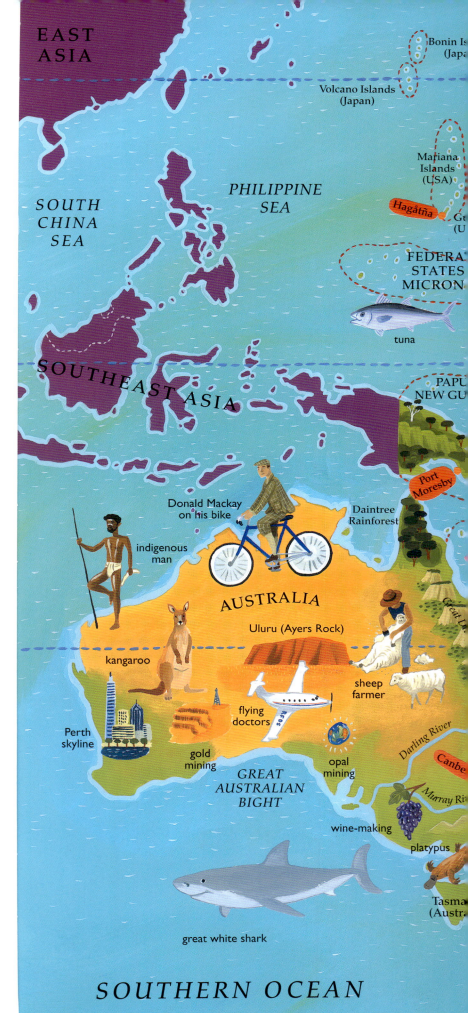

EAST ASIA

Bonin Is (Japan)

Volcano Islands (Japan)

Mariana Islands (USA)

SOUTH CHINA SEA

PHILIPPINE SEA

Hagåtña

Gu (U

FEDERAL STATES MICRON

tuna

SOUTHEAST ASIA

PAPU NEW GU

Port Moresby

Daintree Rainforest

Donald Mackay on his bike

indigenous man

AUSTRALIA

Uluru (Ayers Rock)

kangaroo

sheep farmer

Perth skyline

flying doctors

gold mining

opal mining

GREAT AUSTRALIAN BIGHT

Darling River

Canbe

Murray Ri

wine-making

platypus

Tasma (Austra

great white shark

SOUTHERN OCEAN

Hawaiian Islands (USA)

Tropic of Cancer

Polynesian
outrigger

Wake Island
(USA)

surfer

Mauna Kea
Observatories

Johnston
Atoll (USA)

PACIFIC OCEAN

manta ray

MARSHALL
ISLANDS

Palikir

Delap-Uliga-Djarrit

king bird
of paradise

Howland Island (USA)

Line Islands

Equator

Baker Island (USA)

Bairiki

Yaren

NAURU

KIRIBATI

Vaiaku

TUVALU

SOLOMON
ISLANDS

split
drum

green
turtle

Cook
Islands
(NZ)

Honiara

CORAL
SEA

rugby

SAMOA

Apia

VANUATU

Port Vila

FIJI

Suva

American
Samoa
(USA)

TONGA

Niue
(NZ)

dancing girl
with grass skirt

Tropic of Capricorn

New
Caledonia
(France)

horned
parakeet

Nuku'alofa

French
Polynesia
(France)

Coral Sea Islands (Australia)

Norfolk
Island
(Australia)

Kermadec
Islands (NZ)

PACIFIC
OCEAN

Pitcairn
Islands (UK)

Sydney Opera
House

Māori
man

TASMAN
SEA

International Date Line

HMS Bounty

kiwi

Wellington

Southern Alps

NEW ZEALAND

Chatham
Islands (NZ)

Southeast Asia

Asia is the giant among continents. It's the largest piece of the earth's crust to remain above water, and nearly half the world's population lives in just one part of it: a fertile belt running through south, southeast and east Asia.

Physical Features
Southeast Asia includes the world's largest archipelago, a group of 14,000 islands sprinkled across the ocean between the Asian mainland and Australia. Four slabs of the earth's crust meet here, so there are numerous volcanoes, and earthquakes are not unusual.

People and Places
The largest country is Indonesia, which has a population nearly half the size of Europe's, scattered across 6,000 islands. Bangkok is the capital and largest city of Thailand with over 6 million people. In contrast, northern Thailand is rural, mountainous and much less densely populated.

Climate and Weather
As the region straddles the equator, the climate is warm and humid. The island of Borneo is home to one of the world's oldest rainforests. The tropical climate is also excellent for growing crops.

Land Use and Natural Resources
Rice is a staple food of the region and is also exported all around the world. Thailand is the world's largest exporter of rice. Rubber is also shipped overseas, as is timber, palm oil, sugarcane, coffee and tin.

Environment
Over 90% of southeast Asia's rainforest has been felled, mostly for timber and to create space for farming. Rainforest canopies absorb carbon dioxide from the atmosphere, so when the trees are felled, carbon is released, contributing to global warming. Today, more and more people are realising how important it is to preserve the rainforests.

Transport
With so many islands, boats and ships are an important form of transport. The Strait of Malacca is one of the most important shipping lanes in the world, linking the Indian Ocean and the Pacific Ocean.

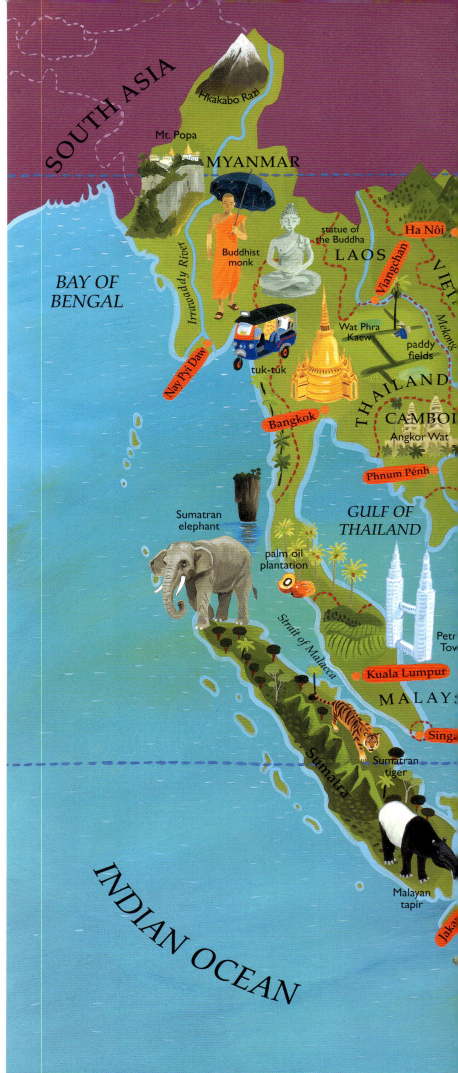

SOUTH ASIA

Hkakabo Razi

Mt. Popa

MYANMAR

statue of the Buddha

Ha Nôi

LAOS

Viangchan

VIET

BAY OF BENGAL

Irrawaddy River

Buddhist monk

Mekong

paddy fields

Wat Phra Kaew

Nay Pyi Daw

tuk-tuk

THAILAND

CAMBO

Bangkok

Angkor Wat

Phnum Pénh

Sumatran elephant

GULF OF THAILAND

palm oil plantation

Strait of Malacca

Petr Tow

Kuala Lumpur

MALAYS

Sing

Sumatra

Sumatran tiger

Malayan tapir

INDIAN OCEAN

Jak

EAST ASIA

Did You Know?

Equator

SOUTH
CHINA
SEA

Vietnamese
cyclist

PHILIPPINE SEA

PACIFIC OCEAN

Banaue
rice
terraces

Manila

Luzon

PHILIPPINES

Palawan

SULU
SEA

Sultan's
Palace

BRUNEI   orchid

Bandar Seri Begawan

Mt. Kinabalu

Mindanao

jeepney bus

RUBY

PALAU

Koror

CELEBES
SEA

Rajang River

dwarf cuscus

Halmahera

sulphur-crested
cockatoo

Tropic of Capricorn

Sulawesi

butterflies

Borneo

orang-utan

knobbed
hornbill

Makassar Strait

Buru   Seram

West Papua
(Indonesia)

JAVA SEA

Mt. Semeru

Balinese
dancer

INDONESIA

tree
kangaroo

fee
ation

Java

Bali

Lombok

komodo
dragon

Sumbawa   Flores

Dili

EAST
TIMOR

ARAFURA
SEA

Borobodur

Sumba

West
Timor

TIMOR SEA

East Asia

Everything in east Asia is on a grand scale, from the Great Wall of China to the vast Gobi Desert and the high-altitude Tibetan plateau.

Physical Features

China is an extremely varied land, with mountains, steppes, plateaus and deserts in the west and a vast fertile plain in the east. To the east of China lie the Korean peninsula and the islands of Japan, both of them largely mountainous.

People and Places

At 1.3 billion people, China is the world's most populated country, accounting for a fifth of the world's population. The Han Chinese, who make up 92% of the population, form the largest single ethnic group in the world. Much of Japan is densely populated, and its capital, Tokyo, is the world's largest city with a population of 27 million.

Climate and Weather

The countries of east Asia have hot, wet summers and dry, cold winters. Temperatures in the mountainous regions of west China are far cooler than those in the south and east.

Land Use and Natural Resources

Although it has the largest agricultural output in the world, only 15% of China's total land area is cultivated. The main crop here, as in Japan and Korea, is rice. All three countries are major producers of manufactured goods.

Environment

As it changes from a rural to an industrial economy, the way China generates energy is becoming critical to the management of global warming. Around 80% of its electricity comes from coal, but it is exploring more sustainable forms of energy production, including solar power plants in the deserts and offshore wind farms. Japan has been leading the world in pollution reduction since the 1970s with electric trains, a focus on clean, efficient engines and strict anti-pollution laws.

Transport

Japan is one of the most technologically advanced countries in the world and is home to the iconic 'shinkansen', the bullet train which travels at speeds of up to 300kph. China's growing economy is bringing rapid increases in car ownership.

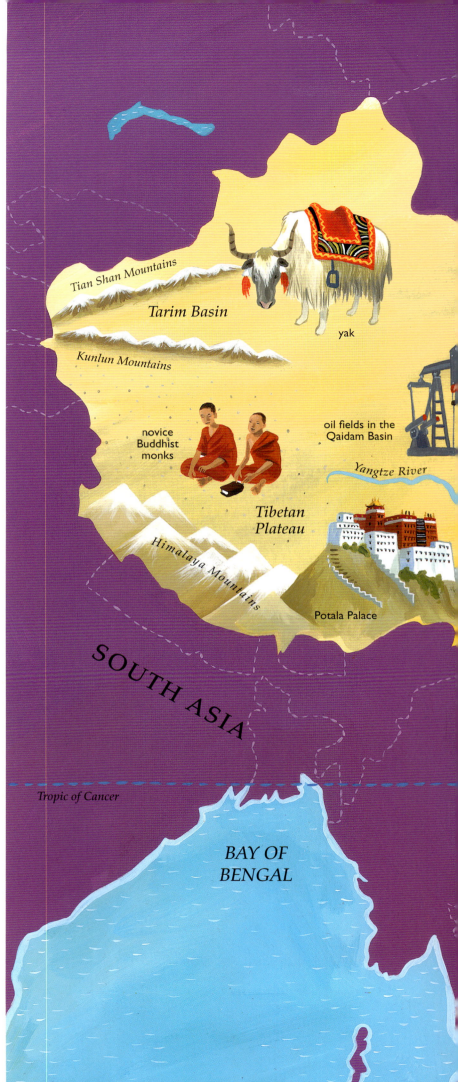

Tian Shan Mountains

Tarim Basin

yak

Kunlun Mountains

oil fields in the Qaidam Basin

novice Buddhist monks

Yangtze River

Tibetan Plateau

Himalaya Mountains

Potala Palace

SOUTH ASIA

Tropic of Cancer

BAY OF BENGAL

NORTH ASIA

coal mining

Japanese crane

SEA OF OKHOTSK

Gobi Desert

Changchun car manufacturing

Mt. Baekdu

NORTH KOREA

tae kwon do

SEA OF JAPAN

Tokyo skyscrapers

Great Wall of China

Beijing

P'yŏngyang

Seoul

bullet train

CHINA

Forbidden City

sapphire

SOUTH KOREA

Hwaseong Fortress

JAPAN

Tokyo

panda

Yellow River

Oriental Pearl Tower, Shanghai

torii gate

bamboo forest

children playing table tennis

Three Gorges Dam

Yangtze River

jade

Donghai Bridge Wind Farm

EAST CHINA SEA

golden monkey

rice paddies

T'aipei

Did You Know?

Hong Kong skyline

TAIWAN

pineapple

Chinese junk

SOUTHEAST ASIA

SOUTH CHINA SEA

North Asia

North Asia includes the world's largest country, the Russian Federation, and one of the world's remotest landscapes, the Gobi Desert, in Mongolia.

Physical Features
This region is home to some of the harshest environments on Earth including wide expanses of frozen tundra, deserts which stretch across Mongolia and the high, remote volcanoes of the Kamchatka peninsula in eastern Siberia.

People and Places
Although nearly twice the size of the United States, the Russian Federation only has half its population. Moscow is the region's most populous city with over ten million inhabitants. At the other extreme, many people in the Arctic regions remain semi-nomadic, tending large reindeer herds which provide much of their food and wealth.

Climate and Weather
Because the Russian Federation extends so far north, the climate can be harsh. In winter, temperatures in Siberia, a region east of the Ural Mountains, can fall to -60°C. The town of Oymyakon claims to be the coldest inhabited place on Earth.

Land Use and Natural Resources
Due to the harsh climate and landscape, less than one-tenth of Russia is cultivated. Most people live west of the Ural Mountains on a vast, fertile plain used for growing cereals like wheat and barley. The Russian Federation is the planet's fossil-fuel giant. It has the world's largest natural gas reserves, the second-largest coal reserves and the eighth-largest oil reserves. Russia has so much fossil fuel that 55% of its energy comes from natural gas, and only 5% from nuclear.

Wildlife
The Russian Federation is a sanctuary for some of the rarest animals on the planet, including the snow crane and the Siberian tiger.

Transport
The majority of Russian personal and cargo transport is by train, as the road system is not extensive and often in disrepair. There are many urban rapid-transit systems as well as the Trans-Siberian Railway which has 9,000km of track.

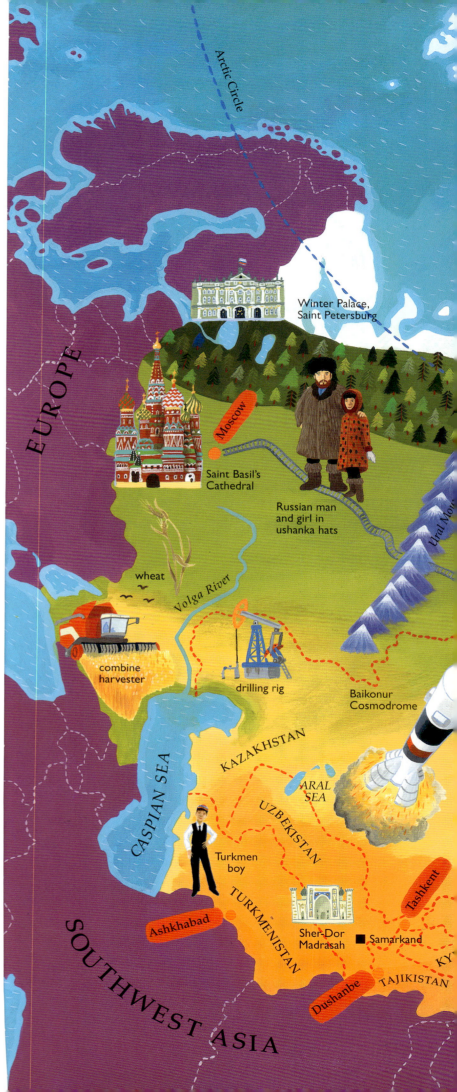

Arctic Circle

Winter Palace, Saint Petersburg

EUROPE

Moscow

Saint Basil's Cathedral

Russian man and girl in ushanka hats

Ural Mou...

wheat

Volga River

combine harvester

drilling rig

Baikonur Cosmodrome

KAZAKHSTAN

CASPIAN SEA

ARAL SEA

UZBEKISTAN

Turkmen boy

Tashkent

Ashkhabad

TURKMENISTAN

Sher-Dor Madrasah

Samarkand

KY...

Dushanbe

TAJIKISTAN

SOUTHWEST ASIA

ARCTIC OCEAN

BERING
SEA

snow crane

Arctic Circle

walrus

reindeer

Oymyakon ■

brown bear

volcanoes of
Kamchatka

SEA OF
OKHOTSK

Siberian
Plateau

coal mining

Ob' River

Urengoy
gas field

Yenisey River

RUSSIAN
FEDERATION

Lena River

Siberian tiger

fisherman's hut

Trans-Siberian Railway

Vladivostok

ana

Genghis Khan

Ulan Bator

Gobi
Desert

MONGOLIA

Mongolian
camel

yurt

k

EAST ASIA

South Asia

This is one of the most heavily populated parts of Asia. Its landscapes range from low, fertile plains to the heights of the Himalayan peaks.

Physical Features

Around 70 million years ago, this section of the earth's crust collided with east Asia, pushing up folds of rock to form the Himalayas. Among them is Mount Everest, the highest mountain in the world at 8,848m. In 1953, Edmund Hillary and Tenzing Norgay made the first successful ascent of Mount Everest.

People and Places

Three-quarters of a billion people in this region rely on river water which comes from melting ice and snow in the mountains. India is the largest country in the region, and the second most populous country in the world, after China.

Climate and Weather

Southern parts of the region have hot summers and monsoon rains while the Himalayas are snow-capped all year round. Pakistan experiences some of the most extreme temperatures on Earth, ranging from 50°C in the south in summer to -50°C in the northern mountain ranges in winter.

Land Use and Natural Resources

Afghanistan is largely mountainous, with just 15% of the land suitable for farming. At the mouth of the Rivers Brahmaputra and Ganges is Bangladesh, where the soil and climate are so favourable for agriculture that farmers often harvest three crops a year.

Environment

The average Indian is very 'green', emitting just 1 ton of carbon dioxide per year through burning fossil fuels, compared to 20 tons per year for the average American and 46 tons for a person living in Qatar.

Wildlife

This region is home to many rare species, among them the Bengal tiger, the Asiatic lion, the snow leopard, the one-horned rhinoceros and the Indian elephant. The Indian elephant is a subspecies of the Asian elephant and is the largest land animal in Asia.

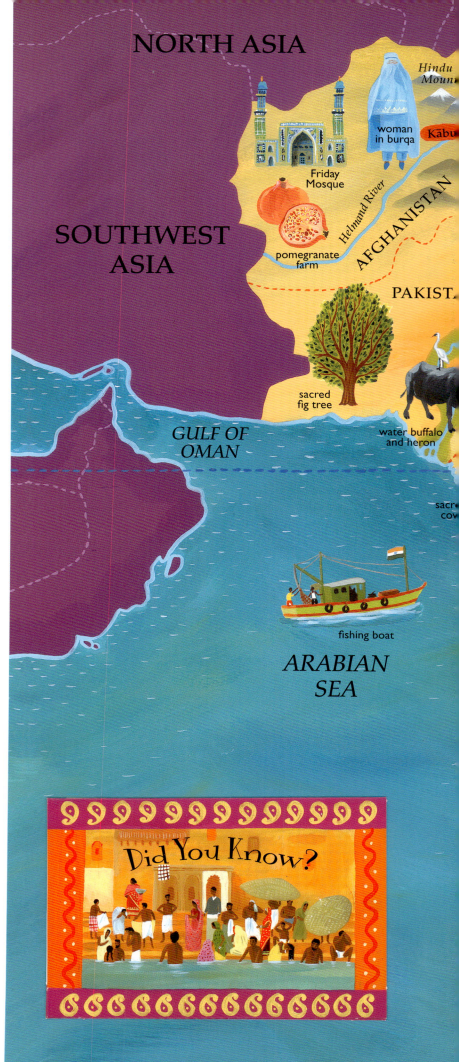

NORTH ASIA

Hindu Moun

woman in burqa

Kabu

Friday Mosque

Helmund River

AFGHANISTAN

SOUTHWEST ASIA

pomegranate farm

PAKIST.

sacred fig tree

water buffalo and heron

GULF OF OMAN

sacre cow

fishing boat

ARABIAN SEA

Did You Know?

EAST ASIA

Karakoram Mountains

snow leopard

Islamabad

Lahore Fort

Golden Temple

New Delhi

woman carrying water

Thar Desert

Mehrangarh Fort

Taj Mahal

blue houses of Jodhpur

INDIA

Himalaya Mountains

NEPAL

Mt. Everest

Kathmandu

Edmund Hillary

Thimphu

BHUTAN

INDIA

Brahmaputra River

tea pickers

bathers in the Ganges

Ganges River

Bengal tiger

Dhaka

boy playing cricket

BANGLADESH

Tropic of Cancer

SOUTHEAST ASIA

Satpura Range

Bombay stock exchange

Indian peacock

General Post Office, Kolkata

BAY OF BENGAL

Deccan Plateau

Gateway of India

Ambassador car

tuk-tuk

banyan tree

Lakshadweep (India)

Chennai temple

Indian elephant

Andaman Islands (India)

Sri Lankan girl

Nicobar Islands (India)

SRI LANKA

Sri Jayewardenepura Kotte

Sri Lankan stilt fisherman

INDIAN OCEAN

Malé

THE MALDIVES

Southwest Asia

Southwest Asia (also known as the 'Middle East') lies at a continental crossroads between Asia, Europe and Africa.

Physical Features

Most of this region is desert, yet within it are the snowcapped Caucasus and Alborz mountains, and the world's largest body of enclosed water, the Caspian Sea. The Rub' al Khali is the world's largest expanse of sand.

People and Places

The world's first civilisation took root in what is now Iraq in the 6th millennium BCE. Between the Tigris and Euphrates Rivers, the Sumerian people built great cities surrounded by fields and orchards. Much of Iran is a vast plateau over 1,000m high and ringed with mountains. Tehran is the largest city in southwest Asia, with a population of 15 million.

Climate and Weather

Most of southwest Asia is either arid or semi-arid, so drought is an increasing challenge. Temperatures in Saudi Arabia can reach up to 54°C in summer. At the other extreme, the summit of Mount Damāvand, the highest peak in Iran at 5,671m, remains snow-capped all year round.

Land Use and Natural Resources

Saudi Arabia is by far the biggest country in the region and has one-fifth of the world's oil reserves. Combined with Iran, Qatar and the United Arab Emirates (UAE), the region has the greatest proven reserves of natural gas in the world after the Russian Federation.

Environment

Some of the world's most astonishing cities are found in southwest Asia, such as Dubai, which is home to the Burj al Arab, the fourth-tallest hotel in the world. Carbon emissions in southwest Asia are by far the highest in the world — a person in the UAE on average emits 15 times more than a person in China.

Wildlife

Species found in southwest Asia include cheetahs, lynx, lizards, turtles, whales and dolphins. The rarest bird in the region is the northern bald ibis, which is critically endangered, but some have recently been discovered in Syria.

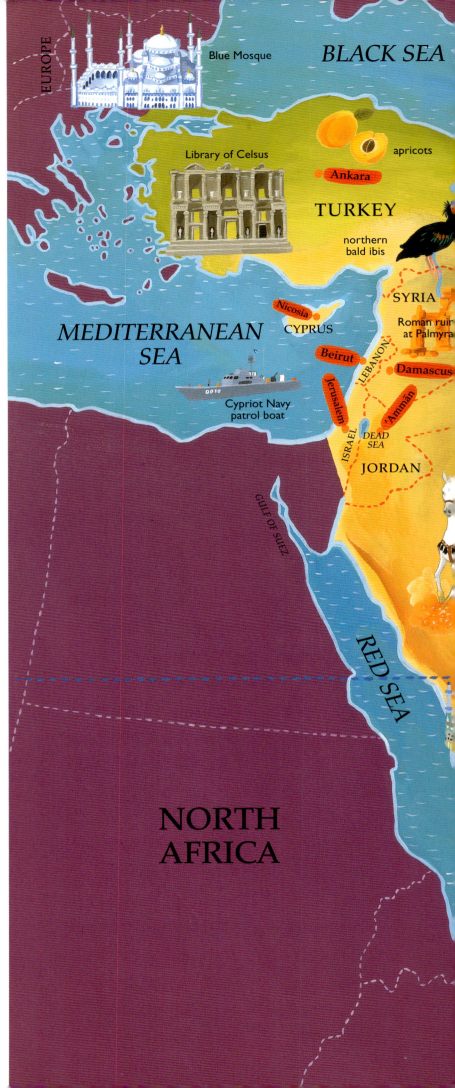

EUROPE

Blue Mosque

BLACK SEA

Library of Celsus

apricots

Ankara

TURKEY

northern bald ibis

Nicosia

CYPRUS

MEDITERRANEAN SEA

SYRIA

Roman ruin at Palmyra

Beirut

LEBANON

Damascus

Jerusalem

ISRAEL

DEAD SEA

Ammān

JORDAN

Cypriot Navy patrol boat

GULF OF SUEZ

RED SEA

NORTH AFRICA

Caucasus Mountains

CASPIAN SEA

...ari ...stery

GEORGIA

T'bilisi

ARMENIA

AZERBAIJAN

Yerevan

Baki

Did You Know?

Alborz Mountains

Mt. Damāvand

Eurasian lynx

Great Mosque of Samarra'

Euphrates River

Tigris River

Zagros Mountains

Tehrān

Baghdād

IRAN

Shah Mosque

kestrel

...am Ali Mosque, Najaf

IRAQ

...abian ...rse

KUWAIT

Kuwait

SOUTH ASIA

Iranian girl

oil fields

Burj Al Arab Hotel

SAUDI ARABIA

Al Manāmah

BAHRAIN

QATAR

PERSIAN GULF

Doha

GULF OF OMAN

Riyadh

UNITED ARAB EMIRATES

Abu Dhabi

Muscat

Tropic of Cancer

OMAN

Mecca

Rub' al Khali

Omani man

Arabian fishing boat

frankincense tree

figs

date palms

YEMEN

Old Walled City of Shibam

Arabian dhow

ARABIAN SEA

Şan'ā'

GULF OF ADEN

Europe

The second-smallest continent on the planet is an intricate jigsaw of 43 countries inhabited by 580 million people who speak 35 different languages.

Physical Features
With its many peninsulas and seas, Europe has an extraordinarily long coastline, which varies in character from deep Norwegian fjords to the sandy beaches of Greece and great river deltas like the Danube. Inland, there are many mountain ranges, including the Alps and Carpathians, which together stretch for 2,000km across the heart of the continent. About 25% of the land area of the Netherlands is below sea level, so has to be protected from flooding.

People and Places
Some of the world's most famous cities, such as Athens, Rome, Paris and London are found in Europe. About three-quarters of Europeans live in or around cities, which often sprawl out into smaller suburbs. The largest of these cities is Paris in France, home to around 10 million people and the famous Eiffel Tower. Europe includes several countries that are so small that they cannot even feature on a map of this scale, such as Andorra, Liechtenstein, Monaco and San Marino.

Climate and Weather
Europe has a wide range of climates because its northern edge reaches far beyond the Arctic Circle while its southern boundary almost touches Africa. Northern Scandinavia has an alpine tundra climate and temperatures in Iceland have reached a record low of −37.9°C, though the Gulf Stream warms it considerably. This Atlantic current also affects the rest of Europe, making it generally warmer than other regions at this latitude. Southern Europe's Mediterranean climate is one of warm, dry summers and mild, wet winters.

Land Use and Natural Resources
Much of Europe is richly fertile and has historically been excellent for the cultivation of crops. These range from olive groves in the Mediterranean south to more frost-tolerant cereals and pulses in central and northern countries. France is well known for its fields of lavender. Some parts of the region are also rich in coal.

Environment
It was Europeans who drove the change from making things by hand to making them with machines. Known as the Industrial Revolution, this 'machine age' marked the start of a sudden increase in fossil-fuel emissions, which contribute to global warming. Europeans are now trying to decrease their harmful emissions. Germany has taken the lead in developing solar power. Austria and Sweden generate about half of their electricity from hydropower. Denmark produces a higher proportion of its electricity from wind power than any other country and manufactures around half of all wind turbines worldwide.

Did You Know?

Wildlife
Animals such as reindeer and moose live in the Arctic north, while in the Mediterranean south there are heat-loving animals including snakes and scorpions. Wild boars, also known as wild pigs, inhabit much of northern and central Europe. If caught unawares, they can be quite aggressive in their behaviour.

Transport
Europe is one of the easiest regions to travel around, as most places are accessible by rail, road, air or sea. Steam-powered rail transport originated in England in the 1800s and the rail network has now expanded to include the entire European continent. The Channel Tunnel runs under the English Channel and connects the United Kingdom to the rest of Europe's rail system. Europe also has some of the world's busiest airports and seaports.

North Africa

Africa is the second-largest continent in the world, with over 50 countries, a population of about one billion and around 2,000 languages.

Physical Features

The Sahara is the largest desert on Earth, covering 9,000,000km². It is expanding southwards at an average of 0.8km per month. The desert is not all sand, but includes gravel plains, salt flats and mountains.

People and Places

Most of the people in north Africa live near the coasts or on the banks of rivers. In Egypt, 90% of the population lives on the banks of the Nile River and on its enormous delta.

Cairo is the largest city in Africa, with a population of 18 million. By comparison, only 2 million people inhabit the Sahara Desert. The largest country is Sudan, with over 100 languages and around 570 different ethnic groups.

Climate and Weather

North Africa has the hottest place in the world: the highest temperature ever recorded was 57.8°C in El Azizia, Libya in 1922. Half of the Sahara receives less than 20mm of rain per year, whereas some of the highest of the Tibesti Mountains receive as much as 120mm annually.

Land Use and Natural Resources

Historically, the countries of northern Africa have followed small-scale farming methods. Much of the land has been depleted by war and by over-cultivation from occupying powers. Some countries, like Algeria, Libya and Nigeria, have large oil reserves.

Environment

Africa is the continent that is most vulnerable to the impacts of climate change as it will get even hotter due to global warming. However, the average African burns far less fossil fuel than most people on the planet.

Transport

The Nile River has been used as a transport route for people and goods for over 2,000 years. The Trans-Sahara Highway, from Algiers to Lagos, is one of the oldest and most complete transnational highways in Africa.

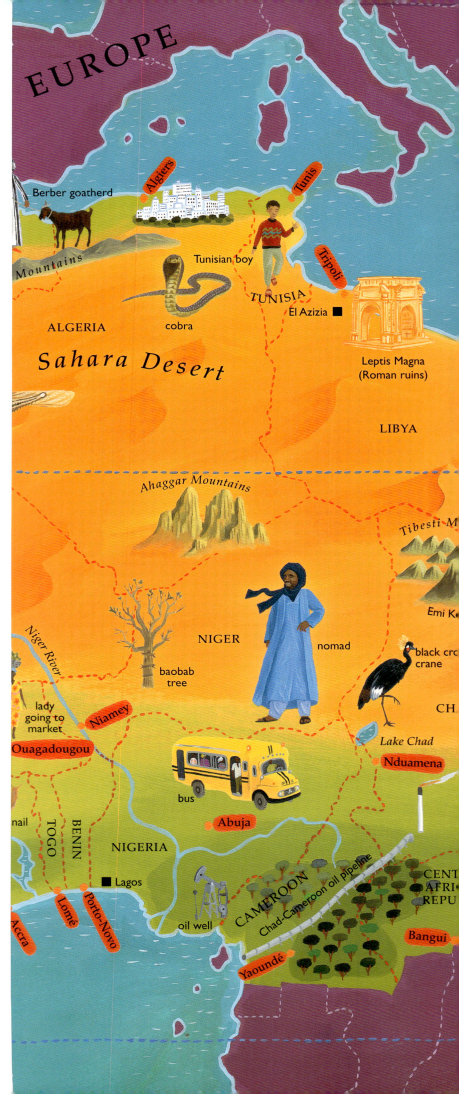

EUROPE

Berber goatherd

Algiers

Tunis

Mountains

Tunisian boy

Tripoli

TUNISIA

El Azizia

ALGERIA

cobra

Leptis Magna
(Roman ruins)

Sahara Desert

LIBYA

Ahaggar Mountains

Tibesti M

NIGER

nomad

Emi K

black cr
crane

baobab
tree

CH

lady
going to
market

Niamey

Lake Chad

Niger River

Ouagadougou

Nduamena

bus

nail

TOGO

BENIN

Abuja

NIGERIA

Lagos

CAMEROON

CENT
AFRI
REPU

Lomé

Porto-Novo

Chad-Cameroon oil pipeline

Accra

oil well

Bangui

Yaoundé

BLACK
SEA

CASPIAN SEA

MEDITERRANEAN SEA

SOUTHWEST ASIA

PERSIAN GULF

Cairo skyline

Cairo

Suez Canal

pyramids

ancient
Egyptian

dates

EGYPT

scorpion

felucca
boat

Jebel Barkal

Nile River

RED SEA

Tropic of Cancer

Sudanese
children

Burj
Al-Fateh
Hotel

gazelle

Asmara

ERITREA

Blue Nile

White Nile

Khartoum

martial
eagle

Djibouti

GULF OF ADEN

Arabian dhow

The Church
of St. George

DJIBOUTI

SUDAN

baboon

Nile crocodile

ETHIOPIA

SOMALIA

Addis Abeba

Ethiopian Highlands

African wild dog

SOUTHERN
AFRICA

Mogadishu

Southern Africa

Southern Africa is a region of extraordinary contrasts and great cultural diversity. It is considered to be the birthplace of man.

Physical Features

The landscapes of Southern Africa range from rainforests, immense rivers and spiky mountain ranges to fertile farmland and deserts. At 5,895m, the highest mountain on the continent is Mount Kilimanjaro in Tanzania.

People and Places

At the tip of the continent is South Africa, the wealthiest country in the region. Cape Town, the legislative capital of South Africa, is overlooked by Table Mountain. The indigenous people of the Kalahari Desert, the San Bushmen, speak a unique 'click' language.

Climate and Weather

The varied climate of southern Africa includes arid, hot deserts and wet, lush rainforests. In contrast, there are still glaciers at the summit of Mount Kilimanjaro, though scientists have predicted that these will have melted by 2020.

Land Use and Natural Resources

Countries in the east of the region were the first to domesticate coffee, sorghum and watermelon. In the west, staple crops include yams and rice. The Congo Basin provides fresh water, food and shelter to 75 million people, but it is under threat from logging, hunting, farming and mining. The rest of the world needs the Congo Basin too, because its vast rainforest soaks up carbon dioxide.

Environment

The region's biggest consumer of energy is South Africa, which has a lot of sunshine but no oil reserves. To help fulfil their energy needs, many South Africans use solar water heaters. Solar-powered traffic lights have been installed at some Cape Town road intersections. South Africa also has about 280,000 windmills, second only to Australia.

Wildlife

The Congo Basin is the world's second-largest tropical rainforest and is home to many species, from mountain gorillas to rare butterflies. In Tanzania, the Serengeti boasts the largest seasonal migration of nearly 2 million herbivores.

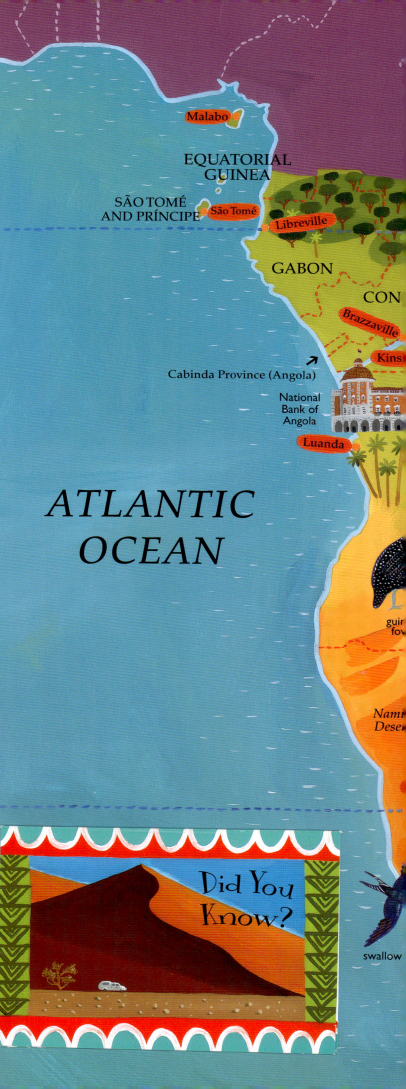

Malabo

EQUATORIAL GUINEA

SÃO TOMÉ AND PRÍNCIPE   São Tomé

Libreville

GABON

CON

Brazzaville

Kins

Cabinda Province (Angola)

National Bank of Angola

Luanda

ATLANTIC OCEAN

guin fow

Nam Dese

Did You Know?

swallow

NORTH AFRICA

INDIAN OCEAN

Equator

SEYCHELLES

Congo Basin

Congo River

gorilla

De Brazza's monkey

UGANDA

Great Rift Valley

Samburu warrior

KENYA

Kampala

Lake Victoria

tea picking

Mt. Kenya

DEMOCRATIC REPUBLIC OF CONGO

RWANDA

Kigali

Nairobi

Mt. Kilimanjaro

Riyadha Mosque

Bujumbura

BURUNDI

Serengeti

okapi

TANZANIA

Dodoma

Pemba

Zanzibar

Victoria

woman carrying water

Stanley and Livingstone

giraffe

fishing boat

diamonds

safari vehicle

COMOROS

tomato frog

ANGOLA

Moroni

ring-tailed lemur

ZAMBIA

MALAWI

Lake Malawi

zebra

lion

Lusaka

Lilongwe

cichlid fish

Zambezi River

Harare

Victoria Falls

hippopotamus

Catholic church

MOZAMBIQUE

MOZAMBIQUE CHANNEL

Antananarivo

MAURITIUS

San Bushmen

BOTSWANA

ZIMBABWE

Port Louis

MIBIA

Réunion (France)

Kalahari Desert

Limpopo River

coconut

MADAGASCAR

Tropic of Capricorn

African elephant

rice terraces

Gaborone

Maputo

rugby players

SOUTH AFRICA

Mbabane

SWAZILAND

gold

Maseru

LESOTHO

Table Mountain

Cape Town skyscrapers

Cape Town

North America

The Americas are named after the Italian explorer Amerigo Vespucci, although Christopher Columbus and John Cabot are often credited as the first European 'discoverers'. This region is a melting pot of nationalities despite being made up of only two countries, Canada and the USA.

Physical Features

North America has a spectacular variety of physical features, from forests, grasslands and deserts to glaciers and mountains. The Rocky Mountains stretch 4,800km from British Columbia in Canada to New Mexico in the USA. The longest river on the continent, the Mississippi-Missouri, starts in the Rockies and flows for 5,969km to the Gulf of Mexico. In between lies a huge swathe of flat grassland, steppe and prairie that makes up the 'Great Plains' of the Midwest.

People and Places

The largest country in north America is Canada. It is also the second-largest country in the world, yet it has less than 1% of the world's population. Washington is home to the White House, the official residence of the President of the United States.

For centuries, North America was inhabited by a wide variety of native peoples. Then, between 1820 and 1910, many millions of immigrants, most of them from Europe, settled in the USA and Canada. Much of Quebec, in eastern Canada, was settled by French colonists and it remains a largely French-speaking province.

Climate and Weather

North America has many different climatic zones, from the cold Arctic coast to the hot and sunny south. The east coast of the United States is relatively mild and humid; the west coast has a warmer, drier climate. Canada is cooler, with a polar climate above the Arctic Circle.

The region experiences some very destructive weather, including hurricanes on the Atlantic and Gulf coasts, damaging wind cyclones in the Midwest's Tornado Alley and devastating wildfires in the west coast's dry climate.

Queen Elizabeth
Islands

gyrfalcon

musk ox

Victoria
Island

purple saxifrage

Baffin Island

BAFFIN BAY

Inuit
kayaker

DAVIS STRAIT

Arctic Circle

Canada
goose

buffalo

HUDSON
BAY

Arctic
hare

harp
seal

ice
hockey
player

NADA

moose

Belcher
Islands

logging

Newfoundland

grain elevator

maple
tree

CN
Tower

Château
Frontenac

Prince
Edward
Island

lobster

ATLANTIC
OCEAN

Missouri River

wheat

The Great
Lakes

Ottawa

Niagara
Falls

Statue of
Liberty

UNITED
STATES OF
AMERICA

cherries

the White
House

Washington

Mount
Rushmore

American
football
player

cotton

space
shuttle

oil
fields

Mississippi River

peanuts

Rio Grande River

paddle steamer

alligator

MEXICO,
'RAL AMERICA
THE CARIBBEAN

GULF OF
MEXICO

Mexico, Central America and the Caribbean

Though these countries are part of the North American continent, their culture is very distinct from the USA and Canada.

Physical Features

Stretching south from the USA into the tropics, Central America is a tapering tail of land forming a narrow bridge into South America. Facing it across the Caribbean Sea is an arc of 7,000 or so islands, islets and reefs. The region sits on the junction of several of the earth's crustal plates, forming several mountain ranges and volcanoes. The Panama Canal is a 77km ship canal joining the Atlantic and Pacific Oceans, replacing the long and treacherous route around the tip of South America.

People and Places

Central America's unique character can be traced back to the mixing of the European conquistadors and the indigenous peoples. Over half of the 190 million people in this region live in Mexico, with an astonishing 20 million gathered in the greater part of Mexico City, which is the largest city in the region. Belize is the only country in this area with English as its official language.

Climate and Weather

The weather can vary between extremes with wet weather from June to October and dry weather from November to May.

Land Use and Natural Resources

The landscape ranges from arid desert to lush rainforest. Most of the economy is based on agriculture, with maize, wheat and rice being the main cereal crops. On the mainland, there are many cattle ranches, providing beef for export. The biggest Caribbean island, Cuba, is the world's third-largest producer of sugar.

Environment

Cubans generate electricity by burning the leftovers from sugarcane factories. In the capital, Havana, thousands of Cubans grow organic vegetables in tiny urban plots known as 'organopónicos'. Mexico has one of the largest geothermal power-producing areas in the world, which supplies energy to the United States and Belize.

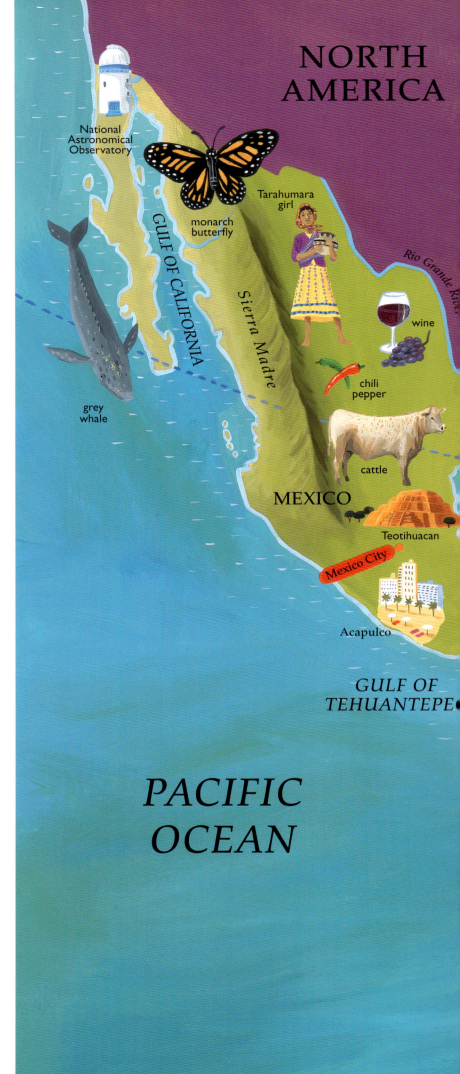

NORTH AMERICA

National Astronomical Observatory

GULF OF CALIFORNIA

monarch butterfly

Sierra Madre

Tarahumara girl

Rio Grande River

wine

chili pepper

grey whale

cattle

MEXICO

Teotihuacan

Mexico City

Acapulco

GULF OF TEHUANTEPEC

PACIFIC OCEAN

ATLANTIC OCEAN

Did You Know?

Bermudian boy

Bermuda (UK)

GULF OF MEXICO

oil rig

Tropic of Cancer

Junkanoo parade

THE BAHAMAS

flamingo

STRAITS OF FLORIDA

Havana

Nassau

YUCATAN CHANNEL

conquistador

bamboo

CUBA

tobacco plant

Turks and Caicos Islands (UK)

rhinoceros iguana

British Virgin Islands (UK)

Anguilla (UK)

San Juan

ANTIGUA AND BARBUDA

keel-billed toucan

coffee

cactus

vintage car

DOMINICAN REPUBLIC

Puerto Rico (USA)

St. Barthélemy (France)

ST. KITTS AND NEVIS

St. Martin

Belmopan

Rastafarian

JAMAICA

HAITI

Santo Domingo

US Virgin Islands (USA)

Guadeloupe (France)

GUATEMALA

BELIZE

Kingston

Port-au-Prince

Montserrat (UK)

DOMINICA

bananas

loggerhead sea turtle

Martinique (France)

Guatemala City

ST. LUCIA

Guatemala

San Salvador

HONDURAS

CARIBBEAN SEA

BARBADOS

EL SALVADOR

Tegucigalpa

giant anteater

ST. VINCENT AND THE GRENADINES

NICARAGUA

Curaçao (Netherlands)

Bonaire (Netherlands)

GRENADA

Port of Spain

Managua

Aruba (Netherlands)

TRINIDAD AND TOBAGO

red-eyed tree frog

San Salvador Cathedral

COSTA RICA

PANAMA CANAL

Panama City

San José

PANAMA

SOUTH AMERICA

container ship

GULF OF PANAMA

South America

Nowhere else in the world do so many humans coexist with such an important natural habitat. South America is home to 374 million people and to over one-third of the world's species of land-based plants and animals.

Physical Features

The Amazon Rainforest is the largest surviving tropical rainforest on the planet, and has been evolving over millions of years. It takes its name from the longest river on the continent, the Amazon, which is also considered by some to be the longest river in the world. The western side of the continent is dominated by the Andes, the longest mountain range in the world. The highest peak is Aconcagua at 6,959m, which has a number of glaciers. It is the highest mountain outside Asia.

People and Places

The population of South America is a combination of native peoples and settlers from southern Europe, largely Portugal and Spain, who came to the continent in the eighteenth century. In the Amazon region, there are 60–90 tribes who have had no contact with the outside world. There are only about 100 uncontacted tribes worldwide. Today, over three-quarters of South Americans live in towns and cities. São Paulo, in Brazil, has more inhabitants than New York and is the most populous city in the Americas.

Climate and Weather

West of the Andes, the climate shows dramatic contrasts – the Atacama Desert in Chile is the driest in the world whereas northern Colombia is one of the wettest regions in the world. Northeast of the Andes, much of the continent's climate is tropical, but southeast of the mountain range, the climate is much cooler and often windy.

Land Use and Natural Resources

The fertile pampas, or grasslands, of Argentina are used to rear beef cattle and cultivate wheat. Cattle are also raised in northern Colombia and Venezuela. In Brazil, coffee is a major crop, and so is sugarcane, which is converted to biofuel. Brazil is also the largest producer and consumer of sugar in the world.

South America is rich in fossil fuels. Colombia has vast coal reserves, while Venezuela's oil makes it the richest country in the region. Flowing northwest in the Pacific from southern Chile to northern Peru, the Humboldt Current has helped to create the most abundant marine ecosystem in the world, as well as the largest fisheries including anchovies and sardines.

Did You Know?

Environment

The Amazon Rainforest accounts for over half of the world's remaining rainforest and covers 1.4 billion acres. The size of the rainforest is being reduced due to logging and farming. In addition to the staggering loss of plant life, many animal species are declining due to habitat loss caused by logging and farming. The rainforest is also sensitive to climate change. Scientists predict that if the earth's global temperature increases by 4°C, up to 85% of the rainforest could be lost.

Wildlife

One in ten of all known species and one in five of all bird species are found in the Amazon Rainforest. Around 3,000 species of freshwater fauna have been found in Amazonia and scientists think there may be as many as 6,000 more species waiting to be discovered. Among the many other varied species of the Amazon are over 1,000 types of frogs, including the poison dart frog. Of the 1,500 species of birds found in the Amazon Rainforest, the red-and-green macaw is one of the most striking, but its numbers are declining due to habitat loss.

Glossary

atmosphere: The mixture of gases that surround the earth.

carbon balance: The balance between the amount of carbon released into the atmosphere and the amount that is stored in the oceans, the soil and vegetation. For example, felling the trees of the rainforests creates an imbalance; planting trees helps to restore it.

carbon emissions: The release of carbon into the environment in gaseous form, in particular by heating and lighting, industrial processes, agriculture and transportation.

'clean' energy: Energy that is generated in a way that does not pollute the atmosphere.

climate: The prevailing weather conditions over a time period, including temperature, precipitation (rain, hail or snow) and wind speeds.

climate change: The change in climate over time. Climate change can be caused by natural cycles and events, and by the greenhouse gas emissions of humankind.

conservation: The management of the natural environment in such a way that wildlife and plants are protected from damage or extinction.

diverse/diversity: Made up of many different, interconnecting elements, like pieces of a puzzle. The earth is defined by its diversity because it is home to many varying forms of life, each of which depends on the others for its existence.

ecosystem: A community of interacting plants and animals, small and large, within their particular environment.

environment: The surroundings and conditions in which a person, plant or animal lives.

fossil fuel: Fuels found underground, which have been formed from the fossilisation of living things like plants and animals. The main fossil fuels are petroleum, natural gas, coal and peat.

geothermal: Relating to the internal heat of the earth. In volcanic areas, it can be used as an energy source.

global warming: The increase in temperature of the earth's atmosphere.

'green': A way of describing the activities and philosophy of those concerned with protection of the environment.

greenhouse effect: The trapping of the sun's warmth in the earth's lower atmosphere. The release of carbon dioxide from burning fossil fuels into the atmosphere contributes to a 'greenhouse effect', which leads to global warming.

greenhouse gas: A gas that contributes to the greenhouse effect by absorbing infrared radiation.

habitat: The place where a plant or animal lives.

hemisphere: Half of the globe.

hydropower: The generation of electricity from flowing water.

natural resource: A material or living being that occurs or exists naturally on Earth without human technology.

projection: The representation of a three-dimensional object on a flat surface. We use projections to create maps.

radiation: Energy emitted in the form of waves or particles, including the energy given off by the sun.

sustainability: The ability to use natural resources in such a way that they are not depleted.

threatened species: A species that is in danger of becoming extinct in the near future.

Sources

Clover, Charles. *The End of the Line: How Over-fishing is Changing the World and What We Eat.* London: Ebury, 2004.

Dow, Kirstin and Thomas E. Downing. *The Atlas of Climate Change: Mapping the World's Greatest Challenge.* Earthscan Atlas Series. London: Earthscan, 2011.

Encyclopedia of Animals. London: Dorling Kindersley, 2006.

Fortey, Richard. *The Earth: An Intimate History.* London: HarperCollins, 2004.

Geographica: World Atlas and Encyclopedia. Potsdam: H.F. Ullmann, 2008.

Girling, Richard. *Rubbish!: Dirt on our hands and crisis ahead.* London: Eden Project, Eden Project Books, 2005.

Hulme, Mike. *Why We Disagree About Climate Change: Understanding Controversy, Inaction and Opportunity.* Cambridge: Cambridge University Press, 2009.

Kunzig, Robert and Wallace S. Broecker. *Fixing Climate: The story of climate science – and how to stop global warming.* London: Green Profile, 2008.

Pearce, Fred. *The Last Generation: How nature will take her revenge for climate change.* London: Eden Project Books, 2006.

Pollan, Michael. *The Omnivore's Dilemma.* London: Penguin, 2006.

Rahmstorf, Stefan and Katherine Richardson. *Our Threatened Oceans.* London: Haus, 2007.

Roberts, Callum. *The Unnatural History of the Sea: The Past and Future of Humanity and Fishing.* London: Gaia Books Ltd., 2007.

The Times Comprehensive Atlas of the World. London: HarperCollins, 2005.

Walker, Gabrielle and Sir David King. *The Hot Topic: How to Tackle Global Warming and Still Keep the Lights on.* London: Bloomsbury, 2008.

Wilson, Edward O. *The Diversity of Life.* London: W. W. Norton, 1993.

Worldwatch Institute. 2009 *State of the World: Confronting Climate Change.* London: Earthscan Ltd., 2008.

Index of Countries and Capitals

Barefoot Books

294 Banbury Road

Oxford, OX2 7ED

Text copyright © 2011 by Nick Crane

Illustrations copyright © 2011 by David Dean

Graphic design by Louise Millar, London

Cartography by Stephen Raw, Manchester

Reproduction by B & P International, Hong Kong

Printed in Malaysia

This book was typeset in Fligerish, Minya Nouvelle, Palatino and Rockwell

The illustrations were prepared in acrylics

ISBN 978-1-84686-332-5

British Cataloguing-in-Publication Data:

a catalogue record for this book is available from the British Library

1 3 5 7 9 8 6 4 2

Editor's Note: As there are many different ways to spell and name the places of the world, for consistency we conformed to the spellings in *The Times Comprehensive Atlas of the World.*

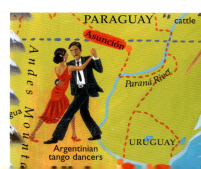